BAKING WITH
MRS BUN THE BAKER
REVISED & EXPANDED

HELLO

Whatever age you are 2 or 92, when you make something, a sense of pride is achieved. It's something you can share with others and be proud of – and this is particularly true of baking.

This book gives children an insight into how exciting baking can be and will inspire confidence in adults who have never baked before. You just need some basic kitchen equipment, some every day ingredients and you'll be away.

The recipes have been tried and tested in my regular cooking classes for all ages (from toddlers to adults). They're easy to follow, simple to make and can be made in just over an hour. There's also no need for pans on the hob, you only need to bake in the oven.

Dip in and out as often as you like but, most importantly, I hope you enjoy these recipes and have some fun in the kitchen. Happy baking!

Mrs Bun the Baker

BEFORE YOU BAKE

WASHING HANDS

Our hands do everything and go everywhere. Because of this they pick up lots of germs. So we must wash our hands with hot, soapy water before we cook – to wash all the germs down the sink.

APRONS

Aprons are good for keeping your clothes, and your food, clean. They also make a great cloth for wiping your hands (you can just put it in the wash afterwards). Wearing an apron is very important.

HAIR

If you have long hair, it is a good idea to tie it back. It could fall into the food, and that's plain yucky!

SURFACES

It's a good idea to wipe down surfaces before you use them, just to make sure they are super-clean. And always clean up afterwards!

EQUIPMENT

You don't need any fancy equipment. Most of what you will be in your kitchen cupboards already. Here is your checklist of some basics:

- BAKING TRAY
- BUN TIN
- CHOPPING BOARD
- CLOCK or TIMER
- CUTTERS
- GRATER
- GREASEPROOF PAPER
- JUG
- KNIFE and FORK
- MIXING BOWL
- OVEN GLOVES
- PLASTIC BAGS
- ROLLING PIN
- SCALES
- SCISSORS
- SPOONS: teaspoon; tablespoon; wooden spoon
- WHISK

RECIPES

SNACKS

BREAKFAST ROLL UPS 8

SAVOURY ECCLES 12

CHEESE STRAWS and SAUSAGE ROLLS 14

HOMITY PIES 16

PARATHA 18

SPRING ROLLS 20

CHEESY BISCUITS 22

POTATO TORTILLA 24

PICNIC PIES 26

FALAFEL SAUSAGE ROLLS 28

OODLES OF NOODLES SALAD 30

MAINS

PIZZA and DOUGH BALLS 34

RAINBOW TART 38

CHICKEN PIES 40

RATATOUILLE BAKE 42

ENCHILADAS 44

GARDEN COUSCOUS and FLAT BREADS 46

LASAGNA 48

CURRY IN A HURRY 50

ROASTED FETA TARTS 52

STUFFED JACKETS 54

ORZO VEGGIE BAKE 56

SWEETS

MIX 'N' MATCH PUDDING 60

STRAWBERRY RIPPLE ICE-CREAM 62

SURPRISE CHOCOLATE BISCUITS 64

ST CLEMENT'S CHEESECAKE 66

FRUITY KEBABS 68

UPSIDE DOWN CRUMBLE 70

BAKEWELL CAKES 72

CHOCOLATE GINGER LOAF 74

ANZAC BISCUITS 76

MAIDS OF HONOUR 78

BANANA & CHOCOLATE LOAVES 80

SHAPED BISCUITS 82

BREAKFAST ROLL UPS

These are really tasty for breakfast, or you could have them for brunch, take them for a packed lunch, or a picnic, but I think breakfast is best!

You can always make them the night before, if you don't have time in the morning, and warm them through in the oven when you want to eat.

They are great fun to make; I call it painting and decorating!

INGREDIENTS

200g SELF-RAISING FLOUR

50g BUTTER

100ml FULL FAT MILK

TOMATO PURÉE: 3–4 tablespoons

3 RASHERS OF COOKED BACON

50g CHEESE: grated

MUSHROOMS: thinly sliced

HOW TO MAKE

1. PREPARATION

Preheat the oven to gas 4 or 180°C (fan 160°C).

Line a baking tray with greaseproof paper.

2. MAKE THE DOUGH

Place the flour into a bowl.

Chop the butter into cubes and add it to the flour.

Pick up some flour and butter and rub it between your fingertips (as though you are trying to get rid of something that's stuck). Keep rubbing the mixture between your fingertips until it starts to look like breadcrumbs.

Add half the milk and mix well with a spoon.

TIP: Always add liquid slowly – you can always add more if needed. Adding too much is hard to correct.

Add the rest of the milk and mix well until you have a soft, doughy mixture.

TIP: The dough should fall away from your hands, not leave them sticky.

Roll...

4. START PAINTING AND DECORATING

Using the tomato purée tube, squeeze a face onto the pastry.

Now, with the back of the spoon or a knife, spread the purée face all over the pastry, edge to edge – no white bits allowed!

Rip up the bacon, using your fingers, and sprinkle it over the dough.

Sprinkle over some grated cheese and thinly sliced mushrooms.

What a masterpiece you have created!

3. ROLL THE DOUGH

Tear the dough into 2 equal halves.

Sprinkle some flour over your work surface, place a piece of dough on top, sprinkle with a little more flour, and roll.

TIP: Turn your dough as you roll to stop it sticking and flatten the sides which may not be rolling down.

Keep the sides as straight as possible to create a rectangle 30 x 18 cm with a thickness of ½ cm.

Make a face

Art!

continues over the page ▶▶

SNACKS **9**

Rollin'

Rolled

5. ROLL UP! ROLL UP!

Take the edge nearest to you, tuck it in tightly and start rolling it up.

You should have a long Swiss-roll or sausage shape.

6. GET COOKING

Cut this sausage shape into 4–6 thick rings (use your knife like a saw to cut through).

Place them ring side up on a baking tray.

Cook in the preheated oven for 20 minutes.

TIP: Whilst they are cooking, use the rest of the dough to make the next lot, then by the time you have done that – hey presto! – those first breakfast rolls will be ready. And if they get eaten quickly some more will be popping out of the oven.

VARIATIONS

Have them for lunch – replace the bacon with ham.

Want a stacked breakfast roll? Use baked beans instead of the tomato purée and add some sliced sausage.

Try a vegetarian option, with cheese, olives, peppers and spring onions.

Try a dessert one, with chocolate spread, nuts and raisins.

Cuttin'

To the oven!

Eat me

SNACKS 11

SAVOURY ECCLES

Eccles cakes are a favourite sweet treat of mine, but I decided to do a savoury version. (One mum was very excited to hear her daughter had made some Eccles cakes with me, but a little puzzled when she bit into one to discover it wasn't sweet!) For a great snack, son Bun loves them in his packed lunch box.

INGREDIENTS

½ BLOCK OF PUFF PASTRY (250g): take out of the fridge 30 minutes before you start

2–3 COOKED BROCCOLI FLORETS

1 SPRING ONION

HANDFUL SPINACH LEAVES

3 CHERRY TOMATOES

75g RICOTTA CHEESE

40g CHEDDAR CHEESE: grated

HOW TO MAKE

1. PREPARATION

Preheat the oven to gas 6 or 200°c (fan 180°c).

Line a baking tray with greaseproof paper.

2. ROLL THE PASTRY

Sprinkle some flour over a worktop and place the puff pastry on the top.

Flour again over the top and roll out the puff pastry to ½ cm in thickness.

Using a 10 cm circular cutter cut out 5 circles.

TIP: Keep the cutter to the edge and the circles close together to achieve the most circles.

Reroll the remaining pastry and cut 2 more circles, then roll for 1 more circle.

You will now have 8 circles.

Roll

Fill

Turn

3. CHOPPING

Chop up the cooked broccoli – the floret and stalk.

Using scissors, cut the spring onion up.

TIP: Wash your hands after chopping the onion as it can be strong and if you wipe your eyes, it can sting.

Tear up the spinach into tiny pieces.

TIP: It is thin so tearing spinach is like tearing paper.

Chop the tomatoes in half, and in half again; make sure you can get all those seeds in too!

Put all these ingredients in a bowl.

4. BIND IT TOGETHER

Add the ricotta and cheddar cheeses to the bowl.

Mix everything up until it's all sticking together.

5. MAKE THE CAKES

Lay the 8 circles of puff pastry out on a worktop.

Place some mixture in the middle of each circle.

Brush egg or water around the edge of the circles.

Lift the edges and squeeze them together.

6. READY TO COOK

Turn the Eccles cakes over.

Make 2 slits in the top of each and place them on a baking tray.

Bake them in the preheated oven for 18–25 minutes.

VARIATION

Use mincemeat for a traditional sweet Eccles cake.

CHEESE STRAWS AND SAUSAGE ROLLS

I find these so much tastier than shop-bought cheese straws; they are moist, flaky and – I promise you – you will want to come back for more.

The sausage rolls are great for toddlers (no raw meat involved as they do like to taste test!).

INGREDIENTS

½ BLOCK OF PUFF PASTRY (250g): take out of the fridge 30 minutes before you start

100g CHEDDAR CHEESE: grated

6 COOKED COCKTAIL SAUSAGES

HOW TO MAKE

1. PREPARATION

Preheat the oven to gas 6 or 200°c (fan 180°c).

Line a baking tray with greaseproof paper.

2. ROLL THE PASTRY

Cut the puff pastry block in half and squash the blocks down with your fingers to soften the pastry.

Sprinkle the work surface with flour.

Place one half of the pastry on the surface and sprinkle the top with a little more flour.

Use your rolling pin to create a 25 x 25 cm square.

TIP: Don't worry if you don't have it exactly the right size, or if the edges are wonky.

3. ADD CHEESE AND FOLD

Scatter the grated cheese over the left half of the rolled-out pastry – make sure you sprinkle it all the way to the edges.

Fold the empty right side over onto the cheese side.

Seal the edges together with your finger tips.

Fold the pastry in half again (this time from top to bottom – not right to left).

Strips

4. STRIPS

Roll out this cheesy pastry to a 14 x 14 cm square.

TIP: Again, don't worry about wonky sides.

Cut the pastry into strips (each 2 cm wide).

Take each end of the strip and twist them around.

Lay them on the baking tray.

Place them in the preheated oven for 10–12 minutes.

5. THAT OTHER HALF OF PUFF PASTRY!

Roll this pastry into a rectangle about 20 x 15 cm.

TIP: If you have wonky edges this time, you need to cut them straight for our sausage rolls.

Cut the rectangle into 6 even pieces.

6. ADD SAUSAGES

Place a sausage in the middle of each of the rectangles.

Dip your finger in some water, and paint each edge of the rectangle.

Fold each rectangle over a sausage.

TIP: Imagine you are putting the sausage to bed!

Use a fork to press the bottom edges together.

TIP: So the sausage won't pop out of bed!

Place them in the preheated oven for 15 minutes.

To the oven!

SNACKS

HOMITY PIES

Crush

These pies date from World War II, when they were a filling supper – there were no snacks to fill up on in those days! I have made these a little more luxurious and tastier than those wartime ones, and hope you agree they are quite moreish.

INGREDIENTS

½ BLOCK OF SHORTCRUST PASTRY (250g): take out of the fridge 30 minutes before you start

½ TIN OF POTATOES (200g): crushed

2 SPRING ONIONS

2 TABLESPOONS SWEETCORN: frozen or tinned

50g CHEESE: grated

50ml CRÈME FRAÎCHE

2 SPRIGS OF PARSLEY

HOW TO MAKE

1. PREPARATION

Preheat the oven to gas 4 or 180°c (fan 160°c).

You will need 6–8 circular pie dishes (10 cm diameter).

2. ROLL THE PASTRY

Flour a worktop and place the pastry on the top.

Flour again and roll out the shortcrust pastry to ½ cm in thickness.

TIP: Push your rolling pin not just in the middle, but all around, otherwise the middle will be very thin and the outer pastry will be too thick.

Cut out 5 circles (if possible with a 10 cm circular cutter) and place them into the pie dishes.

Keep rolling out the pastry until it is all used up.

You should hopefully have 6–8 pie cases.

Mix

Fill

Eat!

3. MAKE THE PIE FILLING

Drain the potatoes from the tin and place them into a plastic sandwich/freezer bag.

Seal the bag and crush the potatoes with your hands.

TIP: I often use bags for crushing ingredients – you can still feel the textures, but without getting messy hands!

Empty your bag of squashed potatoes into a bowl.

Use some scissors to cut up the spring onions into small chunks.

Add the spring onions, sweetcorn, cheese and crème fraîche into the bowl and mix well.

4. ADD THE PARSLEY

Rip the leaves off the stalks.

Rip these leaves into small pieces and add them to the mix.

5. READY TO COOK

Place tablespoons of the mixture into each pastry case.

Place in the preheated oven for 15–20 minutes until golden brown.

Leave to cool – and enjoy!

VARIATIONS

Use an individual pie dish to make a larger pie – especially good for picnics.

For more colour, chop up red and green peppers and use instead of the sweetcorn.

Use sweet potatoes for added texture. Cook them first, and then use as the tinned potatoes.

PARATHA

Measure

Do you want a change from sandwiches every day? A paratha is an Indian stuffed bread which is usually fried. However, here's a way to cook them without stepping near the hob – bake them!

INGREDIENTS

150g PLAIN FLOUR

1 TABLESPOON VEGETABLE OIL

50ml MILK

50ml WATER

A HANDFUL OF PEAS: frozen

1 SMALL COOKED CARROT: chopped

4 SMALL COOKED POTATOES

1 SPRING ONION

1 TEASPOON GROUND CORIANDER

SEASONING

HOW TO MAKE

1. PREPARATION

Preheat the oven to gas 5 or 190°c (fan 170°c).

Line a baking tray with greaseproof paper.

2. MAKE THE DOUGH

Place the flour into a bowl.

Mix the water, oil and milk together.

TIP: Oil will float to the top as it won't easily dissolve with the milk and water. So mix very well!

Pour the liquid into the flour and mix well using a spoon. Then, using your hands, press it all together.

3. KNEAD THE DOUGH

Sprinkle some flour onto the work surface.

Place the dough on top and knead for 5 minutes.

TIP: Try not to drown the dough with flour; it will get too dry to make the bread.

Place the dough to one side to rest.

18 MRS BUN THE BAKER

4. MAKE THE FILLING

Place the peas, carrot and potatoes into a plastic sandwich bag and squash them all up so it's all mushy. It's great fun popping the peas!

Tip the squashed-up ingredients into a bowl.

Cut the spring onion into small pieces and add to the mixture.

Add the ground coriander and seasoning and mix well.

5. MAKE THE BREADS

Sprinkle some flour over the work surface, place the dough on top, sprinkle on some extra flour, and roll to a 3 mm thickness.

Cut out an even number of 10 cm circles (an even number, as you'll need tops and bottoms).

TIP: If you don't have a 10 cm cutter, use a saucer to cut around – just as good.

Re-roll and cut out the dough until it's all used up.

6. ADD THE FILLING

Share the filling between half of the circles, leaving a 1 cm gap around the edge.

REMEMBER: Use half of the circles as you need the other half for the tops.

7. STICK THE BOTTOMS AND TOPS TOGETHER

Wet your finger with water.

Paint around the edge of the dough with the water on your finger.

Take an empty round and place it over the filling.

Stretch the top round to cover the bottom one.

Seal the edges together lightly with your fingertips.

Carefully roll them a little flatter with a rolling pin.

TIP: Don't press too hard; all the filling will pop out!

Make holes in the top with a fork, so the steam can escape.

Put them on a the baking tray and place in the preheated oven for 15 minutes.

SNACKS **19**

SPRING ROLLS

These rolls are made from filo pastry. Filo pastry is a lot like sheets of paper – although you can't write on it! There are a lot of good fresh vegetables, so plenty of your 5-a-day!

INGREDIENTS

½ PACK OF FILO PASTRY (125g)

1 STICK OF CELERY

1 MEDIUM CARROT

1-2 MUSHROOMS

2 SPRING ONIONS

¼ RED or GREEN PEPPER

1 TEASPOON SOY SAUCE

1 TEASPOON GARLIC PURÉE

75-100g RICE NOODLES

1-2 TABLESPOONS BUTTER: melted

HOW TO MAKE

1. PREPARATION

Preheat the oven to gas 6 or 200°c (fan 180°c).

Line a baking tray with greaseproof paper.

Wash all the vegetables to get rid of soil and germs.

2. CHOP, CUT, SLICE AND DICE

TIP: we need everything small!

Cut the celery into ½ cm chunks.

Grate the carrot – be very careful of your fingers!

Break the mushrooms into small pieces (they are so soft, you shouldn't need a knife).

Cut up the spring onions with some scissors.

TIP: Start with the green end – it's easier to cut.

Cut the pepper into long strips, then dice the strips up (you may find a lot of water comes out – peppers are very juicy).

Place all the prepared vegetables into a bowl.

Veg!

Rollin'

3. CHOP, CUT, SLICE AND DICE

Stir the vegetables (all the colours in the bowl should make it look like a rainbow).

Measure the soy sauce, add with the garlic purée and mix well.

Tear up the rice noodles with your hands and mix those in too.

Melt the butter (in a microwave).

4. BE FRAGILE WITH THE FILO

Take the filo pastry from the wrapper and lay it out.

Cut it in half lengthways.

Pick up 2-3 pieces of the filo pastry and add a tablespoon or two of your vegetable mix.

Fold in the sides of the roll, so the vegetable mixture is tucked in nicely.

Roll the filo pastry up over the vegetable mixture.

Brush the roll with some melted butter.

Repeat until you have 6-8 finished spring rolls.

Put them on a baking tray and place in the preheated oven for 15 minutes, or until golden and crispy.

VARIATIONS

For extra protein, add cooked chicken or prawns.

For a crunchier spring roll, try some beansprouts instead of rice noodles.

For a hotter spring roll, add fresh chilli or grated fresh ginger.

TIP: Wash your hands carefully after handling chilli and ginger and don't rub your eyes or face as they could end up stinging.

CHEESY BISCUITS

Floury, messy hands are a must for this recipe – getting your hands in the ingredients and feeling them is great fun.

These biscuits come in many shapes and sizes: stars, circles, trains, squares – any shaped cutter you have will be fine.

TIP: Playdough cutters are great (a huge array of shapes!) and often cheaper than food cutters.

INGREDIENTS

110g PLAIN FLOUR

75g BUTTER or HARD MARGARINE: leave in the fridge until needed

75g CHEESE: grated (use a strong cheese for flavour)

2–3 TABLESPOONS MILK

SEASONING

HOW TO MAKE

1. PREPARATION

Preheat the oven to gas 5 or 190°c (fan 170°c).

Line a baking tray with greaseproof paper.

2. MAKE THE DOUGH

Place the flour into a bowl.

Chop the butter into cubes and add it to the flour.

Pick up some flour and butter and rub it between your fingertips (as though you are trying to get rid of something that's stuck). Keep rubbing the mixture between your fingertips until it starts to look like breadcrumbs.

Add the grated cheese and season to taste.

Add the milk and mix well with a spoon until it forms a soft ball.

TIP: Always add liquid slowly – you can always add more if needed. Adding too much is hard to correct.

Add a little more milk if it is not sticking together.

Cuttin'

3. TAKE A BREAK

Give the ball of dough a good squeeze (if it is too wet, it will be too soggy to roll out).

Put the ball back in the bowl and place into the fridge for 30 minutes to chill out.

4. MAKE SOME SHAPES

Sprinkle the worktop with some flour and roll out the dough to a thickness of ½ cm and use your cutters to make shapes.

TIP: Cut your shapes close together – the closer they are the more biscuits you'll make.

Re-roll and cut out the dough until it's all used up.

TIP: The dough gets drier each time you re-roll it – cutting your shapes close together also means less re-rolling.

Place the biscuits on the baking tray.

Place them in the preheated oven for 15–18 minutes, or until golden brown.

VARIATIONS

For a spicier biscuit try adding some paprika or chilli powder to the mixture.

Red Leicester or Double Gloucester cheese will give the biscuits a lovely orange colour.

TIP: More cheese won't mean a cheesier biscuit, but a stronger cheese will.

Fresh herbs add taste and colour – chop up and add some chives, rosemary or parsley.

Serve the biscuits with a dip such as guacamole, salsa, tzatziki or houmous.

Eat me

SNACKS 23

POTATO TORTILLA

Crack!

I was inspired to create this from living in Lanzarote. At the end of term the school I taught at would take us all out for a tapas lunch. You had choices of meats, fish, salads and tortillas, in big chunks with a cocktail stick. They were delicious and Mr Bun and I would buy tortilla baguettes to take to the beach. I hope you like them too!

INGREDIENTS

8–10 COOKED POTATOES: either tinned or ones left over from dinner

2 SPRING ONIONS

2 RASHERS OF COOKED BACON

MARGARINE: for greasing

75g CHEESE: grated

3 EGGS

100ml MILK

SEASONING

HOW TO MAKE

1. PREPARATION

Preheat the oven to gas 5 or 190°c (fan 170°c).

You will need a 6-hole muffin tin.

2. MAKE THE MIXTURE

Drain the potatoes from the tin and place them into a plastic sandwich/freezer bag.

Seal the bag and crush the potatoes with your hands.

TIP: I often use bags for crushing ingredients – you can still feel the textures, but without getting messy hands!

Empty your bag of crushed potatoes into a bowl.

Use some scissors to cut up the spring onions and the bacon – you want small pieces.

Add the pieces to the bowl and mix all together.

3. GREASE AND FILL

Dip one of your fingers into some margarine.

Use this finger to grease the holes of a 6-hole muffin tin (this will help the tortillas pop out well).

Spoon the potato mixture evenly into the holes.

Sprinkle some grated cheese over the top.

4. ADD THE EGGS

Crack the eggs into a jug – careful not to get any shell in there.

TIP: A spoon is the best way to get any shell out – your finger can be a little slippery!

Beat the eggs together with a fork, so the yolk and the white are mixed together.

Add in the milk and seasoning and beat again.

Slowly and steadily pour the egg mixture over the potato, onion and bacon mixture until it is covered.

TIP: A jug has a spout so the liquid will pour out easily.

5. READY TO COOK

Place the tortillas in the preheated oven for 20–25 minutes.

Leave them to cool in the muffin cases for a further 15 to 20 minutes before you take them out.

TIP: If you don't do this, they can fall apart from being so hot.

Eat warm or, as I like to eat them, cold!

VARIATIONS

Add some chopped peppers and peas for colour – and for the vitamin C they contain.

Slice the potatoes up instead of crushing and layer them in the muffin cases with the onion in between.

Make a larger version in a round ovenproof dish and slice it into cubes to serve on cocktail sticks.

PICNIC PIES

Filling

These pies are great for picnics or putting in a packed lunch, you can eat them hot or cold. You can also fill them with whatever might be in the fridge.

INGREDIENTS

½ BLOCK OF SHORTCRUST PASTRY (250g): take this out of the fridge 30 minutes before you are going to use it

50–75g CHEDDAR CHEESE: grated

PIE FILLING: of your choice

2 EGGS

150ml MILK

HOW TO MAKE

1. PREPARATION

Preheat the oven to gas 4 or 180°c (fan 160°c).

You will need a 12-hole bun tin or a 20 cm dish.

2. FLOUR YOUR WORKTOP

Shake some flour – it is like snow coming down!

TIP: Don't have an avalanche – you just want a light dusting.

Place the pastry on top.

Sprinkle some more flour over the top of the pastry and roll out the shortcrust pastry to ½ cm in thickness.

3. PASTRY SHAPES

Use a 7 cm circular cutter to cut out circles.

Fit the circles into into a bun tin.

Roll out the pastry until you have enough circles to fill your bun tin, or one large circle for a dish.

Sprinkle the grated cheese on the base of the pastry, making sure they all have the same amount (You don't want some cheesier than others!).

4. CHOOSE YOUR FILLINGS

There are lots of options, for example:

- Ham and sweetcorn
- Tomato and basil
- Bacon (cooked) and tomato
- Tuna and sweetcorn
- Mushroom
- Broccoli (cooked)
- Peppers
- Leeks (cooked)

Choose a filling you would like.

Place a tablespoon of the mixture into each pastry case.

5. CRACK SOME EGGS

Thumbs at the ready (and a jug).

Give the egg a tap on the table. Hopefully you will have made a crack in the egg? If not have another go, but not too hard!

Using your thumbs to make the hole bigger, open up the shell and pour the egg into the jug.

Repeat with the other egg.

6. MIX WITH MILK

Make sure there isn't any shell in the jug.

Mix the eggs with the milk.

TIP: Use a fork so the egg yolk and white mix together.

Pour the egg mixture over the filling. Try not to overfill, you don't want to flood the tin!

7. READY TO COOK

Place the bun tin in the preheated oven for 15–20 minutes until golden brown, or for a 20 cm dish 35–40 minutes

Leave to cool and enjoy.

SNACKS

FALAFEL SAUSAGE ROLLS

Falafels are a firm favourite in the Bun house – with pitta, salad and lots of houmous too. One day I had some mixture that needed using up and some puff pastry, so the falafel sausage roll was born.

INGREDIENTS

½ BLOCK OF PUFF PASTRY (250g): take out of the fridge 30 minutes before you start

½ TIN OF CHICK PEAS (200g): drained

1 LARGE TOMATO

1–2 SPRING ONIONS

75g FETA CHEESE

1 TEASPOON GROUND CORIANDER

1 TEASPOON OF GARLIC PURÉE

SPRIGS OF FRESH PARSLEY

1 EGG: for glazing

Place

HOW TO MAKE

1. PREPARATION

Preheat the oven to gas 6 or 200°c (fan 180°c).

Line a baking tray with greaseproof paper.

2. SQUASHING

Tip the chickpeas into a sieve and wash them under the tap.

Place the chickpeas in a bag and squash them until they are all crumbled up.

TIP: Tie a knot in the bag to stop the chickpeas escaping! Also, take the air out of the bag so it doesn't go 'POP!'

3. CHOPPING

Cut the tomato in half, then in half again, and chop finely.

Cut the spring onion up with scissors.

4. MIXING

Put the chickpeas, tomato and onion into a bowl.

Crumble in the feta cheese.

Add the ground coriander and garlic purée.

Tear the parsley leaves up and add in too.

Mix the filling well.

5. ROLLING

On a floured surface, roll the pastry out to a rectangular shape about 30 x 20 cm.

Place the mixture all the way along the middle.

Brush the edge with egg wash, pull over the top and seal them together.

Cut the long sausage into 8–10 pieces.

6. BAKE!

Put them on a baking tray, brush with egg wash to glaze and place in the preheated oven for 20 minutes.

OODLES OF NOODLES SALAD

We were celebrating Chinese New Year in my cooking class, trying to think of something special to eat and came up with this. Some of the children hadn't come across rice noodles before, but they all loved slurping them up like spaghetti!

INGREDIENTS

¼ OF CUCUMBER

2-3 FLORETS OF COOKED BROCCOLI

3-4 LEAVES OF PAK CHOI or ICEBERG LETTUCE

1-2 TABLESPOONS OF COOKED PEAS

1 COOKED CHICKEN BREAST

125g READY COOKED RICE NOODLES

1-2 FRESH SPRIGS OF MINT AND CORIANDER

1 TABLESPOON OF DRESSING:
for example a mixture of soy sauce, lime juice, sweet chilli sauce and olive oil

HOW TO MAKE

1. CHOPPING

Chop the cucumber and broccoli into small pieces, place in a bowl.

Cut or tear the pak choi or iceberg lettuce and place into the bowl.

Measure the peas out into the bowl.

Cut or tear the chicken into smaller pieces and add it to the bowl.

2. NOODLING!

Place the noodles into the bowl with the other ingredients and mix them all together.

TIP: If the noodles are sticking together, use some scissors to snip them up.

Tear up the mint and coriander and add them to the bowl.

Use your hands to mix it all up.

Eat me

Slurp!

3. DRESS THE SALAD

Mix all the dressing ingredients together in a cup with a spoon.

Pour the dressing over all the noodles. All done!

VARIATIONS

Use Quorn instead of chicken.

If you prefer, leave the dressing off.

PIZZA AND DOUGH BALLS

This is a favourite for the weekend in the Bun household. Make it for tea on a Saturday night instead of ordering a pizza in.

Create your own pizza as you like it, knowing it has been freshly prepared. With this recipe, you even have enough to make some dough balls too.

INGREDIENTS

200g STRONG FLOUR:
use this flour for the stretchy gluten it contains

1 TEASPOON or ½ SACHET YEAST: fast action

PINCH OF SALT

120ml WARM WATER

1 TABLESPOON OF OLIVE OIL

3–4 TABLESPOONS PASSATA

50g MOZZARELLA

See 'Topping' (facing page) for other ingredients

HOW TO MAKE

1. PREPARATION

Preheat the oven to gas 5 or 190°c (fan 170°c).

You will need a pizza tray.

Line a baking tray with greaseproof paper.

2. MAKE THE DOUGH

Place the flour into a bowl.

Add the yeast and salt, and stir together.

Run the tap until you have some warm water

Measure 120ml of water into a jug and add the oil.

Pour the water and oil into the flour and mix well until you have a ball of dough.

3. KNEADING

Knead the dough for 5 minutes on a floured surface.

TIP: Kneading is the stretching, pushing, folding and pressing of your dough in order to make it rise.

Flour

Sauce

4. DOUGH BALLS

Divide the dough into 3 equal-sized pieces.

Pick up one piece and tear it up into 6-8 pieces. (Use these 6–8 pieces to make the dough balls.)

Roll the dough in your hands to make a ball, trying to make it as smooth as possible.

Put them on a small baking tray (a little apart as they are going to rise).

Cover with a tea towel and leave in a warm place to rise for 20–30 minutes.

4. ROLL OUT

Use the 2 remaining pieces of dough to make 2 pizzas, or combine them to make 1 large one.

Place the kneaded dough onto a lightly floured surface and then roll out into 1 large or 2 small circles.

Place the dough circle(s) onto the pizza tray.

5. TOPPING

Spoon the passata over the base, making sure you go all the way to the edges.

Add the toppings of your choice.

For example combine any of the following together:

MEAT: Ham, pepperoni, chicken, cooked bacon, salami, beef, sausages.

FISH: Tuna, prawns, anchovies, mackerel, mussels, shrimps, fish fingers.

VEGETABLES/FRUITS: Tomato, sweetcorn, peppers, mushrooms, olives, pineapple, peas.

Tear up the mozzarella cheese and scatter it over the top.

continues over the page ▶▶

To the oven!

4. BAKE

Place in the preheated oven for 10–15 minutes until golden brown.

The dough balls should have risen now too, so place these in the preheated oven for 8–10 minutes.

VARIATIONS

Have 4 parts to your pizza, making each quarter into a different pattern/flavour.

Use the dough balls for a dessert, serving them with chocolate spread!

Topping

Eat me

Dough balls

MAINS **37**

RAINBOW TART

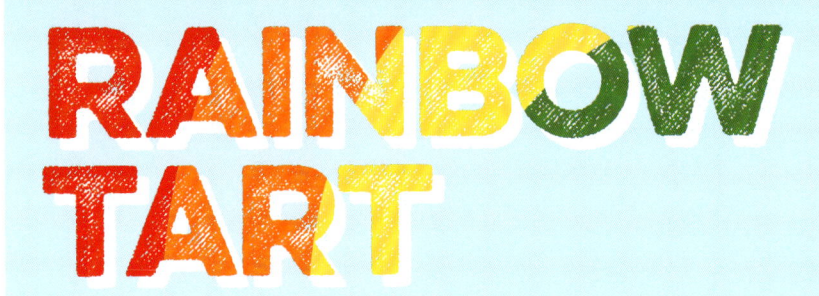

Eggs are so versatile – they make a great snack and contain lots of protein. I like tortillas and Yorkshire puddings, and this recipe combines them both.

INGREDIENTS

¼ PEPPER OF EACH COLOUR:
red, orange, yellow, green

1 SPRING ONION

2 SLICES OF PANCETTA or
2 RASHERS OF COOKED BACON or
2 SLICES OF COOKED HAM

2 EGGS

100ml MILK

75g PLAIN FLOUR

1 TEASPOON GARLIC PURÉE

25g CHEDDAR CHEESE: grated

25g PARMESAN: grated

HOW TO MAKE

1. PREPARATION

Preheat the oven to gas 6 or 200°c (fan 180°c).

Line a 30 x 20 cm Swiss roll tin with greaseproof paper.

2. MAKE A RAINBOW

Use a knife to cut the peppers into long strips.

Chop the spring onion into small pieces.

Use your fingers to tear the meat up.

Lay out all the vegetables and meat in the Swiss roll tin.

3. BREAK AN EGG

Crack the eggs into a jug – be careful not to get any shell in there.

Whisk the eggs together with a fork, until the yolk and the white are mixed up.

4. MAKE A BATTER

Add the milk to the eggs, whisking well.

Next, add the flour, whisking well.

TIP: Sieving the flour will prevent lumpy batter.

Now add the garlic purée to the mix.

5. POUR

Pour the batter from the jug over the rainbow of peppers, onions and meat.

Sprinkle over the cheddar and parmesan cheeses.

6. BAKE

Place in the preheated oven for 15–20 minutes, and watch it puff up!

VARIATIONS

Use a different mixture of vegetables.

Change the meat for Quorn.

MAINS

CHICKEN PIES

Cut

These are great for a packed lunch, and make a good snack, hot or cold. I find my classes cannot get enough of them. It always comes up as a favourite, especially so with the dads – when the children take them home, they are very impressed. I hope you are too.

INGREDIENTS

½ BLOCK OF PUFF PASTRY (250g): take this out of the fridge 30 minutes before you want to use it, so it is softer to roll out

1 SPRING ONION

2-3 COOKED BROCCOLI FLORETS

2-3 SPRIGS OF PARSLEY

2-3 COOKED CHICKEN BREAST SLICES or 1 COOKED CHICKEN BREAST

25g SWEETCORN: frozen or tinned

1-2 TABLESPOONS CONDENSED MUSHROOM SOUP

HOW TO MAKE

1. PREPARATION

Preheat the oven to gas 5 or 190°c (fan 170°c).

Line a baking tray with greaseproof paper.

2. FLOUR YOUR WORKTOP

Sprinkle some flour onto the worktop.

TIP: You just want a light dusting.

Place the puff pastry on top.

Shake some more flour over the top of the puff pastry and roll out to ½ cm in thickness.

3. PASTRY SHAPES

Use a 10 cm circular cutter to cut out circles.

Roll out and cut until you have 8-10 circles of puff pastry.

TIP: Turn the pastry to stop it sticking and cut close together (to get as many circles as possible without re-rolling).

Mixed

Seal

Baked

4. MAKE THE FILLING

Using scissors, cut the spring onion into small pieces.

TIP: Start at the green end and work your way down – you will find it easier.

Cut up the cooked broccoli florets into small pieces.

Tear up the parsley leaves only.

Tear the chicken up into small pieces.

Mix this all together in a bowl. Add the sweetcorn and soup, and mix.

Lay out your pastry circles on the worktop.

Place a teaspoon of the filling into the middle of only half of the circles, leaving a 1 cm edge all the way around.

5. PUT A LID ON IT

Fill a cup half full of water and have your other halves of pastry ready.

Dip your finger into the water.

Dab your wet finger round the edges of the pastry with the filling on.

Place the other half of the pastry on the top.

Using your fingers, or a fork, seal the pies nice and tight, so nothing can leak out.

Place them on the baking tray.

6. READY TO COOK

Use a knife to make a hole in the tops of the pies to let some steam escape.

Place them in the preheated oven for 20 minutes.

Leave to cool and enjoy.

MAINS

RATATOUILE BAKE

I first made ratatouille as a student, in the traditional way with aubergines. I have to admit, I'm not keen on aubergines, so this recipe is an aubergine-free ratatouille – with a lid on!

INGREDIENTS

1 PEPPER: any colour

1-2 CELERY STICKS

½ SMALL COURGETTE

3-4 MUSHROOMS

1-2 SPRING ONIONS

1-2 TABLESPOONS OF OIL

6-8 SMALL COOKED POTATOES

1 TABLESPOON CRÈME FRAÎCHE

HANDFUL OF CHEESE: grated

½ TIN OF CHOPPED TOMATOES (200g)

BASIL LEAVES

Shop! Shop!

Chop! Chop!

HOW TO MAKE

1. PREPARATION

Preheat the oven to gas 6 or 200°c (fan 180°c).

Grease a 15 x 15 cm ovenproof dish or a 2 lb loaf tin.

You will need a baking tray for roasting.

2. CHOPPING

Chop the pepper in half and take out the seeds.

Now chop the pepper into chunks.

Cut the celery into 1 cm chunks.

Slice the courgette into circles of 1 cm thickness then dice.

Using your fingers tear the mushrooms into 4–6 pieces – not too small!

Cut the spring onion up into small pieces.

3. BAKE NO. 1

Place all these ingredients on a baking tray.

Splash the oil over them.

Roast in the preheated oven for 15–20 minutes.

4. POTATO TIME

Whilst the vegetables are roasting, chop the potatoes into slices; they need to be ½ cm thick.

Place the potatoes into a bowl and mix gently with the crème fraîche and grated cheese.

5. BACK TO THE VEG

When the vegetables come out from the oven ask an adult to place them into your ovenproof dish or loaf tin.

Pour in the tomatoes and tear in the basil leaves.

Mix it all together.

6. POTATO TOPPING

Place the mixed potato mixture over the top, trying to cover all the ratatouille below.

If you have extra cheese or some breadcrumbs scatter them over the top for added crunch!

7. BAKE NO. 2

Place in the preheated oven for 20 minutes.

Leave to cool and serve with a green salad.

VARIATION

If you don't like tomatoes leave them out – it's still as good!

MAINS

ENCHILADAS

These are a good introduction to Mexican food, and you can have some great fun making them. Squashing, filling and packing is involved, so you can really get stuck in!

INGREDIENTS

3 SMALL TORTILLA WRAPS

210g TIN OF KIDNEY BEANS: drained and rinsed

1 SPRING ONION

¼ COURGETTE

HANDFUL OF SPINACH LEAVES

2 MUSHROOMS

250ml TOMATO PASTA SAUCE

25g CHEESE: grated

HOW TO MAKE

1. PREPARATION

Preheat the oven to gas 6 or 200°c (fan 180°c).

You will need a 15–20 cm baking dish.

2. MAKE THE FILLING

You will need a sandwich or freezer bag.

Place all the kidney beans in the bag, seal tightly at the top (making sure to squeeze all the air out) and squash the beans in the bag with your fingers.

Cut up the spring onion – start with the green end and work down, then place it in a bowl.

Using a knife cut the courgette into circles, and then cut each round into 4 pieces.

Tear the spinach leaves up – we want small pieces; you will find it is as easy as tearing paper.

Break each mushroom into 6–8 pieces.

Place all these ingredients into the bowl, pour over your pasta sauce and mix well.

Squash

Fill

Wrap

3. PACK THE WRAPS

Lay the 3 tortillas out in front of you.

Place a quarter of the mixture into the middle of each one. (So, at the end, you should have a quarter of the mixture left in the bowl.)

Now wrap them up, like you would a birthday or Christmas present.

Fold in 2 sides to meet in the middle, then fold in the other 2 sides.

Turn them over and place them into the dish, doing the same with the other 2.

With the quarter of the mixture that's left, spoon it all over the wrapped enchiladas and sprinkle with the grated cheese.

Place some tin foil over the top and tuck it all in.

4. BAKE

Place in the preheated oven for 15–20 minutes.

Ask an adult to uncover the enchiladas, then cook for a further 5 minutes.

Serve with a colourful salad.

VARIATIONS

These could be made with some chicken pieces for added protein.

Add some chilli powder for some heat – gradually increase this as you get used to a hot taste!

Serve with some sour cream and guacamole.

MAINS **45**

GARDEN COUSCOUS AND FLAT BREADS

This recipe is perfect if you're growing your own vegetables and herbs so you can use ingredients from your own garden.

INGREDIENTS

100g COUSCOUS

¼ CUCUMBER

6 CHERRY TOMATOES

½ PEPPER

FRESH PARSLEY, CORIANDER and CHIVES

½ TEASPOON GROUND CUMIN

1 TABLESPOON OF OLIVE OIL

SQUIRT OF LEMON JUICE

75g FETA: crumbled

100g SELF-RAISING FLOUR

80g NATURAL YOGHURT

HOW TO MAKE

1. PREPARATION

Preheat the oven to gas 6 or 200°c (fan 180°c).

Line a baking tray with greaseproof paper.

Place the couscous in a bowl and ask an adult to pour 150 ml of boiling water over it. Cover with a tea towel and leave for 10 minutes.

2. CHOP, CUT AND TEAR

Cut the cucumber into 4 strips, then ½ cm chunks.

Cut the tomato in half then, if you would like it smaller, cut these in half again.

Cut the pepper into long strips, and then dice the strips up.

TIP: You may find there is now a lot of water on your board as these ingredients are full of water. It may be helpful to wipe it up or pour it away.

To give your dish flavour, tear all the herbs into smaller pieces.

Place all of these ingredients into a bowl.

3. BACK TO THE COUSCOUS

The couscous should now be ready.

The couscous will have changed into a soft block, so use a fork to break it up.

4. MIXING

Add in the ground cumin, the oil and lemon juice to the couscous and mix.

TIP: Adding these flavours first ensures they're well mixed into the couscous.

Crumble in the feta.

Add in the prepared vegetables and herbs.

Mix well.

5. FLAT BREADS

Mix the yoghurt and flour together.

Squeeze it all together so you have a dough ball.

Sprinkle some flour onto your worktop.

Break the ball into 4–6 pieces, roll them flat (around 10 cm in size) and put them on the baking tray.

Place in the preheated oven for 10 minutes.

Serve with the couscous.

VARIATIONS

Make it more Mediterranean by adding sundried tomatoes and olives.

Add some meat or fish.

Try using giant couscous instead.

MAINS

LASAGNE

Fresh!

When I first made this, Mr Bun thought it was better than the lasagne I used to make the traditional way, with a cheese sauce and a tomato sauce from scratch! It freezes very well too, so you can make batches, thaw out and cook when needed.

INGREDIENTS

HANDFUL OF FRESH SPINACH LEAVES

2 MUSHROOMS

½ RED or YELLOW PEPPER

½ COURGETTE

150ml TOMATO PASTA SAUCE

2 FRESH LASAGNE SHEETS

1 TABLESPOON FULL-FAT SOFT CREAM CHEESE

3 TABLESPOONS OF CRÈME FRAÎCHE

25g CHEESE: grated

HOW TO MAKE

1. PREPARATION

Preheat the oven to gas 6 or 200°c (fan 180°c).

You will need a small ovenproof dish or 2 lb loaf tin.

2. MAKE THE FILLING

Tear up the spinach leaves; remember they are very thin and just melt to nothing when baked!

Rip the mushrooms into 6–8 pieces and place them in a bowl.

TIP: If the mushrooms are dirty, rub off the soil, or just peel the coat off, to show a lovely white shirt underneath!

Use your knife to cut the pepper into strips then into squares.

Chop the courgette: first into circles, then into semi-circles and finally into quarters.

Add the pasta sauce to the vegetables and mix well.

48 MRS BUN THE BAKER

Layer

Spread

3. LAYER THE PASTA AND THE MIXTURE

Place a third of the vegetable mixture in your dish or loaf tin.

Add a lasagne sheet (cut to your dish or tin size).

TIP: You will need to use fresh lasagne sheets. It tears very easily to fit your dish and also cooks quicker than the dried version. Fresh sheets do not take up as much liquid as dry pasta.

You will need to repeat this process 2 times, making sure you finish with a lasagne sheet.

4. FINISHING OFF

Mix the cream cheese and crème fraîche together in a bowl.

Spread this mixture over the top of the final lasagne sheet.

Sprinkle over grated cheese for a golden brown top.

Cover the dish with foil, and tightly tuck all around.

5. BAKE

Place in the preheated oven covered for 15-20 minutes.

Ask an adult to uncover the lasagne, then cook for a further 5 minutes.

Serve with a colourful salad.

VARIATIONS

Change the vegetables according to the season.

Add ham and/or pulses for added protein.

CURRY IN A HURRY

This dish is a great way to get youngsters into some stronger, hotter flavours. Keep adding a little more curry powder, then add stronger ones and soon they will want a hot curry!

INGREDIENTS

4 FILO PASTRY SHEETS

1 TOMATO

1 COOKED CARROT

4 SMALL COOKED POTATOES

1 SPRING ONION

HANDFUL OF FRESH SPINACH

STALK OF FRESH PARSLEY

1 TABLESPOON MANGO CHUTNEY

1 TEASPOON CURRY POWDER: mild or medium

HANDFUL OF FROZEN PEAS

HOW TO MAKE

1. PREPARATION

Preheat the oven to gas 6 or 200°c (fan 180°c).

Grease and flour the bottom of a 15 cm round tin.

2. CHOP CHOP

Cut the tomato in half, then quarter, and then dice.

Chop the carrots into pieces about ½ cm thick.

Cut the potatoes in half, then quarter, and then dice.

Use some scissors to cut up the spring onion.

Use your hands to tear up the parsley and spinach into small pieces.

Place all these ingredients into a bowl.

3. MIX

Add in the tablespoon of mango chutney and a teaspoon of curry powder.

Stir in the frozen peas. Mix well.

TIP: Keeping peas frozen will mean they won't go too mushy by being overcooked.

3. FILL THE FILO

Lay 3 pieces of filo pastry into the base of a round dish, with the edges all hanging over.

Pour the mix onto the filo pastry.

Fold the pastry up over the filling.

TIP: If you have a hole in the middle, then scrunch up another piece of filo pastry to cover it.

Place in the preheated oven for 20 minutes.

VARIATIONS

Try these combinations: cauliflower and chickpea; sweet potato and broccoli; squash and peas.

Add a stronger curry powder.

MAINS 51

ROASTED FETA TARTS

This recipe came about from using up leftovers in my fridge, and is now a firm favourite – and lovely with some onion marmalade or chilli jam on top.

INGREDIENTS

½ BLOCK OF SHORTCRUST PASTRY (250g): take out of the fridge 30 minutes before you start

3–4 MUSHROOMS

½ COURGETTE

½ PEPPER

75g BUTTERNUT SQUASH (⅓ of a squash)

1–2 SPRIGS OF FRESH THYME

1–2 TABLESPOONS OF OLIVE OIL

85g FETA: crumbled

HOW TO MAKE

1. PREPARATION

Preheat the oven to gas 6 or 200°c (fan 180°c).

You will need a 12-hole bun tin and a roasting tin.

2. FLOUR YOUR WORKTOP

Shake some flour over your worktop and place the shortcrust pastry on top.

Sprinkle over some more flour and roll the pastry out to ½ cm thickness.

3. PASTRY CIRCLES

Using a 7 cm cutter, cut out enough circles to fill a 12-hole bun tin.

Place the pastry circles in the bun tin.

TIP: Pop the pastry circles in the fridge whilst you prepare the filling. Doing this means the pastry won't shrink when it cooks.

Cut

Fill

Taste!

4. CHOP, CUT AND TEAR

Rip each mushroom into 4–6 pieces.

Slice the courgette into 1 cm thick pieces, then cut those pieces into 4.

Cut the pepper into long strips, then dice the strips.

Cut the butternut squash into pieces that are the size of a dice.

TIP: You may need some help with this – a butternut squash can be quite tough!

5. TIME TO ROAST

Place the vegetables into a roasting tin.

Pick the leaves off the thyme and sprinkle them over the vegetables.

Pour over the oil.

Give the tin a shake and place in the preheated oven for 15 minutes.

6. FILL

Get an adult to take the roasted vegetables out of the oven and place them in a bowl.

Crumble over the feta cheese and mix well

Now place a spoonful of the mixture into each of the 12 pastry cases.

Place the bun tin in the preheated oven for 10–15 minutes.

TIP: The vegetables are all cooked (you are just cooking the pastry now), so when the pastry slides in the tin it means the tarts will be ready.

STUFFED JACKETS

This is such great fun, taking food apart and then putting it back together again!

You can stuff the potatoes with whatever you like and it's a great way to use up leftovers in the fridge.

INGREDIENTS

PRE-COOKED JACKET POTATOES: I found the Maris Piper to be a good baker

COOKED BACON or SAUSAGES

CHOPPED PEPPERS

SWEETCORN

FRESH HERBS: parsley and chives work well

CHEESE: grated

MELTED BUTTER: for taste

SEASONING

Choose as much or as little of the above as you like. See 'variations' for further options

HOW TO MAKE

1. PREPARATION

Preheat the oven to gas 5 or 190°c (fan 170°c).

You need an ovenproof dish to fit 2–3 potato halves.

2. SCOOP

Cut the baked potato in half.

Using a teaspoon, scoop out the potato into a bowl.

TIP: Be careful – you need to leave the potato jacket intact; we don't want to rip it!

3. MAKE THE FILLING

Cut up the bacon/sausages and peppers into small pieces and add to the bowl.

Sprinkle in the sweetcorn.

Chop up your chosen herb(s) and add to the bowl.

Add half of the grated cheese, butter and seasoning.

Mix all together well.

4. PUT IT BACK TOGETHER!

Using a spoon, scoop the filling back into the potato skin halves.

Because we've added more ingredients the skins will be bursting at the seams!

3. BAKE

Place the stuffed potatoes into an ovenproof dish.

TIP: Place them close together, so they support each other and don't fall over.

Sprinkle the remaining cheese over the top. This will make sure they go a golden brown colour and become crispy.

Place them in the preheated oven for 15–20 minutes until golden brown.

Serve with a colourful salad.

VARIATIONS

Breakfast jacket: Use pre-cooked chopped sausages, some baked beans and scrambled eggs.

Roasty jacket: Use up leftover vegetables like broccoli, carrots, peas from your Sunday roast, as well as some of the meat, mix together and fill.

Veggie jacket: Fill with chopped Quorn sausages or mashed-up kidney beans.

Falafel Jacket: Use some falafels mixed with the potatoes and some cheese. Serve with houmous when cooked.

MAINS

ORZO VEGGIE BAKE

5-a-day

This is a great recipe for getting plenty of your 5-a-day – it uses lots of different vegetables!

INGREDIENTS

½ COURGETTE

½ RED PEPPER

3 MUSHROOMS

1–2 SPRING ONIONS

25g SWEETCORN

5–6 BASIL LEAVES

50g ORZO PASTA: Orzo pasta looks like rice grains. If you cannot find this, use any small pasta shapes

150ml PASSATA

100ml WATER

1 TABLESPOON TOMATO PURÉE

HOW TO MAKE

1. PREPARATION

Preheat the oven to gas 6 or 200°c (fan 180°c).

You will need an ovenproof dish – either a 2 lb loaf tin or a 15 cm round dish

2. CUTTING

Make sure all the vegetables are washed to get rid of dirt and germs.

Cut the courgette through the middle lengthways.

Cut these 2 pieces into thin half-moons.

Place the ½ pepper shiny side down and cut it into long strips.

Break each mushroom into about 4-6 pieces.

TIP: Mushrooms are very soft, so soft you can break them up with your fingers.

Using some scissors cut up the spring onion – use all the green and white.

Cut

Pour

3. PUT IT ALL TOGETHER

Place all these vegetables into your dish.

Sprinkle over the sweetcorn.

Tear over the basil leaves.

TIP: Fresh herbs add great flavour to your dishes (you may have them in your garden).

Sprinkle over the orzo pasta and mix well.

Pour the passata into a jug and add in the water.

Now add the tomato purée to the jug and mix together well.

Pour this liquid over the vegetables in the dish.

TIP: Use a jug with a spout so the liquid will pour easily.

4. BAKE

Cover the dish with foil, making sure it is tucked round well.

Place in the preheated oven covered for 30 minutes.

Ask an adult to uncover the dish, then cook for a further 5 minutes.

Leave to stand for 5 minutes before serving.

VARIATIONS

Add a tin of tuna for some protein.

Once cooked, add a spoonful of cream cheese for a creamy tomato sauce.

Vary the vegetables: use grated carrots, even grate the courgette, and add some peas or broccoli.

Spinach is great for extra iron.

SWEETS

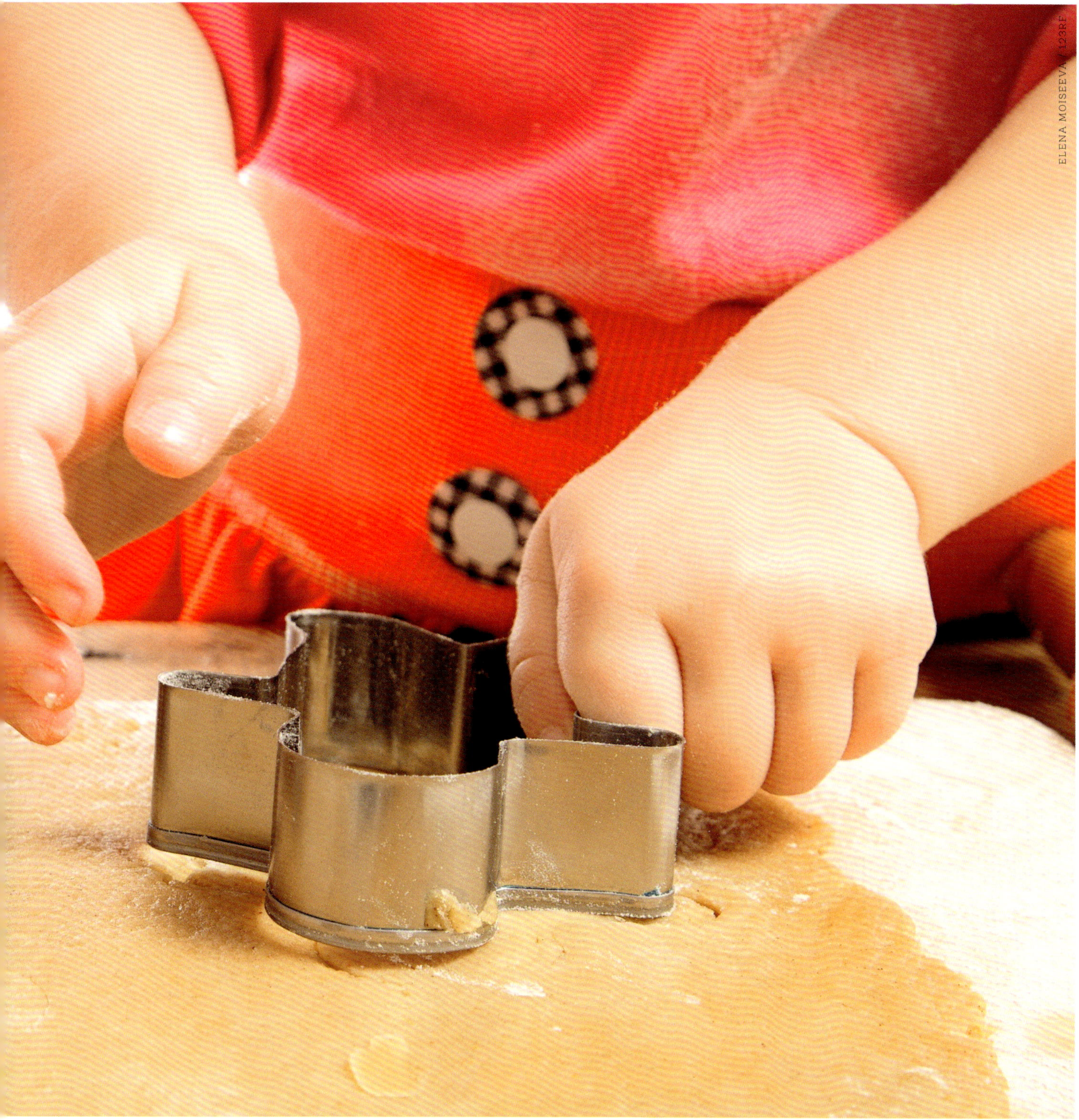

ELENA MOISEEVA / 123RF

MIX 'N' MATCH PUDDING

This is a light sponge with hidden treasures inside. There are many combinations you can choose from but, in the Bun household, we enjoy mixing and matching them. Especially for a good old-fashioned winter pudding.

INGREDIENTS

50g SOFT MARGARINE

25g CASTER SUGAR

1 EGG

50g SELF-RAISING FLOUR

APPLES or PEARS or BANANAS or PEACHES or STRAWBERRIES or DRIED FRUIT

TOFFEE SAUCE or CUSTARD or LEMON CURD or CHOCOLATE SPREAD or JAM

HOW TO MAKE

1. PREPARATION

Preheat the oven to gas 4 or 180°c (fan 160°c).

You will need 3 round 10 cm tins or a round 15 cm ovenproof dish

2. CREAM

Place the margarine in a bowl, then squish and squash it down with a spoon, so it is lovely and soft.

Add in the sugar and mix these together until they stick to the bowl (known as the 'creaming method').

TIP: If you can turn the bowl upside down and the mixture doesn't fall out, you have done well.

3. MIX

Crack the egg into a jug and beat it with a fork.

TIP: To crack the egg give it a tap on the table. If it's not cracked, have another go but not too hard.

Add the egg – slowly – to the sugar and margarine mix, beating well.

4. FOLD

Sieve the flour into the bowl.

Fold the flour into the mixture in a figure of 8.

5. SLICE AND SQUEEZE

Cut the fruit into slices.

Place the slices at the bottom of a baking dish – just enough to cover the bottom.

Pour your chosen sauce/spread over the fruit.

Use a tablespoon and place a good dollop of the mixture on top of the round tins or ovenproof dish.

TIP: There's no need to spread the mixture out as it will melt in the oven.

6. BAKE

Place the baking dish in the preheated oven for 15-20 minutes until golden brown on the top.

Top with cream, ice-cream or more of your sauce/spread.

VARIATIONS

For a chocolate flavour add a tablespoon of cocoa powder to the sponge mix.

Add mixed spice to the sponge.

If you double the mixture you can make an extra big one!

SWEETS 61

STRAWBERRY RIPPLE ICE-CREAM

This ice-cream is very tasty, and came about from another recipe of mine for honeycomb ice-cream. However, strawberries are a much healthier option

INGREDIENTS

15 STRAWBERRIES

225ml DOUBLE CREAM:
use extra thick cream, if you prefer – you don't need to whip it!

100ml SWEETENED CONDENSED MILK

1 TEASPOON VANILLA ESSENCE

75ml SINGLE CREAM

2 TABLESPOONS ICING SUGAR: optional

HOW TO MAKE

1. PREPARATION

You will need a 500 ml freezer-friendly container.

2. SQUISH AND SQUASH

Wash the strawberries and remove their stalks.

Get a strawberry, hold it between your thumb and finger, and squish it into a bowl.

Do the same with all the strawberries.

TIP: Avoid creating big pieces as they will only end up as lumps of ice in the final ice-cream.

3. WHISK

Pour the double cream into a jug.

Whisk the cream until it's sticking to the whisk.

TIP: It should look like ice-cream on top of a cone.

Add in the condensed milk, vanilla essence, single cream and the strawberries.

4. SWIRL

Mix the ingredients up for a ripple effect – but don't over mix or you'll have pink ice-cream with no swirls!

Have a taste. If it's not sweet enough for you add in some or all of the icing sugar.

Squish

Swirl

Eat me

5. FREEZE

Pour the mixture into a 500ml freezer-friendly plastic container.

Place this into the freezer.

Be patient! You will need to leave it for at least 6 hours before you can eat the ice-cream!

TIP: If you take it out 10 minutes before you want it, the finished ice-cream will be easier to scoop.

VARIATIONS

Use other berries such as blueberries, raspberries, blackberries – or use lots of different berries together.

Add some fudge pieces and squeeze in some toffee sauce before it goes in the freezer.

For chocolate-chip ice-cream, add chunks of your favourite chocolate: plain, milk or white. Or, again, mix them together.

Chop and mash a banana for a delicious banana ice-cream.

SWEETS

SURPRISE CHOCOLATE BISCUITS

This is a great mixture as it doesn't require a rolling pin to roll it out, so no mixture sticks to the work surface.

INGREDIENTS

100g MARGARINE

50g ICING SUGAR

125g PLAIN FLOUR

1 TABLESPOON COCOA POWDER

12 WHITE CHOCOLATE CHUNKS

ICING SUGAR/CHOCOLATE: to decorate

HOW TO MAKE

1. PREPARATION

Preheat the oven to gas 4 or 180°c (fan 160°c).

Line a baking tray with greaseproof paper.

2. CREAM

Place the margarine in a bowl, then squish and squash it down with a spoon so it is lovely and soft.

Sift in the icing sugar (sifting gets rid of any lumps in the sugar). Mix with the margarine until you no longer see the sugar.

TIP: Mix the icing sugar in slowly because, if you do it too quickly, it will fly everywhere!

3. FLOUR

Add the flour, spoon by spoon and mix in well.

Add and mix in the tablespoon of cocoa powder.

TIP: The mixture will be crumbly. Squeeze it together in your hands to form a dough ball.

Sift

Count

Jazz up!

4. MATHS!

Cut your ball of dough in half, and then in half again – you now have 4 pieces of the same size.

Break each of the 4 pieces into 3 – you should have 12 pieces of dough.

Roll the 12 pieces into balls.

5. BISCUIT MAKING

Flatten the balls slightly.

Place a chunk of chocolate in the middle of each piece of dough.

Squeeze the dough around the chocolate, to hide it.

Roll the dough back into a ball.

6. BAKE

Place the balls on the baking tray.

Place in the preheated oven for 15–20 minutes.

Take out and leave to cool.

Once cooled sift over some icing sugar, add some chocolate or top with buttercream.

To finish, add some decorations!

VARIATIONS

Use a little piece of fudge inside.

Try a piece of marzipan in the middle.

Decorate with melted chocolate over the top.

For a non-chocolate variation omit the cocoa and add another spoon of flour or some almonds.

SWEETS 65

ST CLEMENT'S CHEESECAKE

This recipe is one of my favourites. It started off with just one flavour, but over the years I have experimented with different ones, and this now is a summery, zesty essential.

My Italian friend Francesco loves this cheesecake, and cannot get enough of it when he visits. Coming from an Italian, this is a HUGE compliment!

INGREDIENTS

100g DIGESTIVE BISCUITS

50g MARGARINE

75ml DOUBLE CREAM

100g CREAM CHEESE

1–2 TABLESPOONS LEMON CURD

250g TIN OF MANDARIN ORANGES: drained or FRESH MANDARINS: if in season

1–2 TABLESPOONS CASTER SUGAR: optional

HOW TO MAKE

1. PREPARATION

You will need 4 small ramekin dishes or a round 15 cm dish.

2. CRUSH!

Place the biscuits into a bag or bowl.

Crush them with a rolling pin.

TIP: Don't bash too hard, the bag may break!

They should look like breadcrumbs when you've finished. (If any big lumps come to the top, give them an extra bash to crush them up.)

3. MIX

Ask an adult to melt the margarine in a microwave.

Pour the margarine into your biscuits and stir.

Pour the mixture into your serving dishes, pressing the biscuits down with a spoon for an even spread.

Place this in the fridge to set.

4. FILLING

Pour the double cream into a bowl and whisk until thick. You will have to be strong to do this!

TIP: Cold cream takes longer to whisk so, to help, take it out of the fridge 30 minutes before.

Whisk the cream until it has gone from being runny to sticking to the whisk.

Stir in the cream cheese and lemon curd.

Mix it all together well and have a taste – if you feel it needs be sweeter add in some or all of the caster sugar.

5. FINAL TOUCHES

Take the biscuit mixture out of the fridge.

Pour the creamy mixture over the biscuit base, spreading it all over.

Use the mandarin segments to decorate the top.

Leave in the fridge for 2 hours to set.

VARIATIONS

Instead of lemon curd, use fresh lemon zest and juice – just a teaspoon will give you plenty flavour.

Use a tin of raspberries in the creamy mix – but make sure you drain the juice off first, otherwise the mixture will be too wet and it won't set.

Try using ginger biscuits instead of digestives — they go well with the zingy lemon flavour.

Serve individual portions by serving it in plastic tumblers or wine glasses. By doing it this way, you can also see all the different layers.

SWEETS

FRUITY KEBABS

Chop

This is a really fun way to eat fruit: like a lolly, but a healthy lolly and it gives you some of your 5-a-day. So many bright colours can be put on the stick – and everyone's will be different.

INGREDIENTS

STRAWBERRIES

BLUEBERRIES

KIWI FRUIT

GRAPES

TINNED PINEAPPLE CHUNKS

APPLE

MELON

SATSUMA

HOW TO MAKE

1. PREPARATION

Wash the fruits to make sure they are clean.

You will need some wooden skewers.

2. PREPARE THE FRUIT

We need to make sure the fruit pieces are an appropriate size. For example, a whole apple is too big, but whole blueberries, strawberries are fine.

Open the tinned pineapple and drain the juice. These are ready to use, as the chunks are already the perfect size.

Cut the melon and peel the satsuma.

TIP: Melons can be large and tricky so you may need to ask for help.

Cut the top and bottom off the kiwi fruit.

Peel the skin off the kiwi, then cut it in half.

Cut those 2 pieces in half, then in half again so you have 8 chunks of kiwi.

5-a-day

Yum!

The apple will need to be cut, cored and diced.

TIP: If you leave the diced apple for a while before making the kebabs, place it in some water with lemon juice to stop it from going brown.

3. GET SKEWERING!

Now it's time to make the kebabs.

Using the pointed end of the skewer, slide the fruit pieces onto the stick in any order you like.

VARIATIONS

Try a traffic light one with green grapes, orange melon and red strawberries, or maybe even create a rainbow!

If you don't have skewers, make a fruit salad pot.

Make a salad version using tomatoes, cucumber, olives, feta and mushrooms.

Kebabs

SWEETS **69**

UPSIDE DOWN CRUMBLE

I had some left over custard one day, and decided to make a crumble, but wondered if it would work upside down (so I could get all my washing up done at once!). And it did!

INGREDIENTS

125g PLAIN FLOUR

50g BUTTER or HARD MARGARINE: leave in the fridge until needed

50g GRANULATED or DEMERARA SUGAR: this gives a lovely crunchy texture to the topping

125ml READY MADE CUSTARD

2 SMALL APPLES

HOW TO MAKE

1. PREPARATION

Preheat the oven to gas 5 or 190°c (fan 170°c).

You will need 4 ramekin dishes or a loaf tin.

2. MAKE A START

Wash the apples.

Pour the ready made custard into the ramekin dishes – it should go up to about 1½ cm.

3. MAKE THE CRUMBLE TOPPING

Place the flour and butter into a bowl.

Pick up some flour and butter and rub it between your fingertips (as though you are trying to get rid of something that's stuck). Keep rubbing your fingertips like this until the mixture looks like breadcrumbs.

Stir in the sugar.

MRS BUN THE BAKER

4. CHOP THE APPLE

Cut the apples in half, then in half again, then dice them into small pieces.

Place the apple pieces on top of the custard.

5. BAKE

Sprinkle the crumble mix over the apples.

TIP: don't press it down or it will become a firm biscuity top, rather than a soft crumble.

Place in the preheated oven for 20–30 minutes.

It's ready to eat – find the custard at the bottom!

VARIATIONS

Crumble a ginger biscuit, a handful of oats or some mixed spice into the crumble mix.

Add dried fruits such as sultanas and raisins to the apple filling.

For an alternative filling try some stewed rhubarb.

BAKEWELL CAKES

This is an alternative cake version of the famous tart. We often make these in class as so many people like them.

INGREDIENTS

100g MARGARINE

50g CASTER SUGAR

2 EGGS

75g SELF-RAISING FLOUR

25g GROUND ALMONDS

WHITE ICING

JAM

GLACÉ CHERRIES

HOW TO MAKE

1. PREPARATION

Preheat the oven to gas 4 or 180°c (fan 160°c).

You will need a 6-hole muffin tin or 12-hole bun tin.

You will need paper cases to fit your tin.

2. CREAM

Place the margarine in a bowl and soften it with the back of a spoon.

Add the sugar, and mix until it sticks to the bowl.

TIP: If you can hold the bowl upside down without the mixture falling out, you have creamed enough.

3. CRACK THE EGGS

Crack the eggs into a jug and beat with a fork.

TIP: To crack the egg, tap it lightly on a table. If it's not cracked, have another go, but not too hard!

Add the eggs slowly to the mixture, beating well after each addition. (Do not add them all at once – you will flood the mixture and it will curdle.)

Scoop

Yum!

4. MIX

Add in the flour and almonds.

Give the mixture a good beat, making sure all the flour and almonds have disappeared.

For a muffin tin place 4 teaspoons of mixture into each paper case; for a bun tin place 2 teaspoons into each paper case.

5. BAKE

Place them in the preheated oven for 15–30 minutes (depending on 6 or 12 cakes).

TIP: The cakes are ready when you touch them and they spring back and when they're golden brown.

6. ICING

Whilst the cakes are baking, squash and squeeze the white icing to make it soft.

Sprinkle the work top with some icing sugar.

Roll out the icing to ½ cm thickness.

Use a cutter to create the number of tops you need.

7. FILL

Once the cakes are out of the oven, leave to cool.

Once cooled, use a teaspoon and scoop a hole from the top of the cake.

Fill the hole with jam and press the top back on.

8. DECORATE

Place a little jam on the top of the cake – this acts like glue for the icing.

Cover the cake with the round of icing.

Dab a cherry in some jam and stick it on top!

VARIATIONS

If you don't like almonds, use all flour.

Add cocoa to the sponge and use chocolate spread instead of jam to make chocolate bakewells

Add zest of lemon to the sponge and use lemon curd instead of jam.

CHOCOLATE GINGER LOAF

This makes a good loaf cake or alternatively bake muffins, both are just as good, and the best part – no added sugar, just sweetened from the chocolate and ginger preserve.

INGREDIENTS

100g CHOCOLATE

100g MARGARINE

175g GINGER PRESERVE

2 EGGS

150g SELF-RAISING FLOUR

HOW TO MAKE

1. PREPARATION

Preheat the oven to gas 4 or 180°c (fan 160°c).

Line a 1lb baking tin with greaseproof paper.

Get ready

Melt

2. MELTING

Break the chocolate into smaller pieces and place in a microwave-friendly bowl with the margarine.

Melt in the microwave.

Ask an adult to take it out for you – it may be very hot – and give it a stir.

TIP: Where there is no microwave, ask an adult to place the chocolate and margarine in a saucepan and melt on a low heat.

3. GINGER

Place the ginger preserve into a bowl.

Add the melted chocolate to the ginger preserve and mix together until all the preserve is broken up.

4. CAKE MAKING

Crack the eggs into a jug and beat with a fork.

TIP: To crack the egg, tap it lightly on a table. If it's not cracked, have another go, but not too hard!

Add the beaten eggs and flour to the chocolate and margarine and mix well.

Pour the mixture into the loaf tin.

5. BAKE

Place in the preheated oven for 40–50 minutes.

TIP: The loaf is ready when a skewer inserted into the centre comes out clean.

VARIATIONS

For a chocolate orange loaf, use marmalade instead of ginger preserve.

SWEETS

ANZAC BISCUITS

I first made these when I was at college, and really liked them, but didn't make them again until I was a teacher. I was teaching 'Rations and the War', so I dug out and dusted off my old A-level recipe book. ANZAC stands for the Australian & New Zealand Army Corps. The women of these countries made them for their brothers/husbands who were stationed in Gallipoli during World War I.

INGREDIENTS

100g MARGARINE

50g SYRUP

1 TEASPOON BICARBONATE OF SODA: dissolved in a little water

100g PLAIN FLOUR

50g GRANULATED SUGAR

75g PORRIDGE OATS

50g DESICCATED COCONUT

HOW TO MAKE

1. PREPARATION

Preheat the oven to gas 4 or 180°C (fan 170°C).

Line a baking tray with greaseproof paper.

2. MAKE THE WET MIXTURE

Place the margarine and syrup in a heat proof bowl.

Heat the bowl in a microwave for 30 seconds.

In a cup, mix the bicarbonate of soda with a tablespoon of water.

Add the contents of the cup to the contents in the bowl and beat well.

3. PREPARE THE DRY INGREDIENTS

Measure out all the dry ingredients: flour, sugar, oats and coconut and place them all into a bowl.

Use your hands to mix them all together.

4. COMBINE

Time for a spoon. Pour the wet mixture over the dry ingredients and stir.

When all the ingredients are coated with the wet mixture, squeeze the whole mixture into a ball.

5. MATHS!

Cut your ball of dough in half, and then in half again – you now have 4 pieces of the same size.

Break each of the 4 pieces into 3 – you should have 12 pieces of dough.

Roll the 12 pieces into balls.

Place the balls on a baking tray.

TIP: Make sure there is some space between them, as they will spread out in the oven.

7. BAKE

Place in the preheated oven for 10–15 minutes. They will flatten out and turn a golden colour.

Leave them to cool on the tray for 5–10 minutes.

VARIATIONS

If you don't like coconut, replace with extra oats.

Using demerara sugar will give a lovely crunch to the biscuits.

You can decorate with drizzles of chocolate over the top.

MAIDS OF HONOUR

Jam tarts are a sweet treat that are very easy to make, but adding a sponge on the top turns them into a lovely treat. Grandma Bun used to make these when I was little; I still love them.

INGREDIENTS

½ PACK OF SHORTCRUST PASTRY (250g): take out of the fridge 30 minutes before you start

3 TABLESPOONS OF JAM

1 EGG

25g CASTER SUGAR

50g MARGARINE

50g SELF-RAISING FLOUR

HOW TO MAKE

1. PREPARATION

Preheat the oven to gas 5 or 190°c (fan 170°c).

You will need a 12-hole bun tin.

2. FLOUR YOUR WORKTOP

Sprinkle some flour – it is like snow coming down.

TIP: Not an avalanche – just a light dusting.

Place the pastry on top.

Shake some more flour over the top of the pastry, then roll it out to ½ cm thickness.

3. PASTRY CUTTING

Use a 7 cm cutter to cut out your circles.

TIP: Always start at the edge of the pastry when cutting and keep cutting close to each round so you get out as many circles out as possible. Reroll the leftovers to get your 12.

Fit the circles into a 12-hole bun tin.

4. FILL

Put half a teaspoon of jam into each pastry case.

5. SPONGE MAKING

Place the egg, sugar, margarine and flour into a bowl and mix!

The mixture should look lovely and smooth.

Place a teaspoon of the sponge mixture on top of the jam. No need to spread, the oven will melt the sponge mix over it for you.

6. BAKE

Place them in the preheated oven for 15–20 minutes.

TIP: You need to get the pastry bottom cooked, so when they come out of the oven ask an adult to nudge the pastry and it should move freely in the bun tin.

VARIATIONS

If you have pastry left, cut out some stars to put on the top.

Use lemon curd for a zesty filling.

Fancy a chocolate one? Add chocolate spread in the middle and a little cocoa to the sponge top.

Use real berries instead of jam (for example, blackberries or raspberries) to cut down on added sugar.

Add some blueberries or raspberries into the sponge mix for a fruity taste.

SWEETS

BANANA & CHOCOLATE LOAVES

These little loaves need no added sugar, they're sweetened by the banana, chocolate and honey.

INGREDIENTS

- 50g BUTTER
- 100g SELF-RAISING FLOUR
- 25-50g CHOCOLATE
- 1 EGG
- 1 RIPE BANANA
- 1 TABLESPOON HONEY
- 1 TEASPOON VANILLA EXTRACT

HOW TO MAKE

1. PREPARATION

Preheat the oven to gas 5 or 190°c (fan 170°c).

You will need 4 mini loaf tins.

2. CRUMBS & CHOCOLATE

Cut the butter into small pieces.

Using your fingertips, rub the butter into the flour, until it looks like a breadcrumb mixture.

TIP: Shake the bowl and, if any lumps come to the top, continue rubbing them into the mixture.

Break the chocolate up into big or small chunks and add them to the flour.

3. CRACK, MASH, MIX

Crack the egg into a jug and beat with a fork.

TIP: Use one thumb to make the crack in the egg bigger then, with the other thumb, open the hole up.

Peel the banana and chop it into slices.

Mash the slices with a fork.

Place the mashed banana into the jug with the egg.

Measure in the tablespoon of honey and the vanilla essence and mix them all together.

Peel

Mash

Mix

Divide

4. COMBINE

Mix the egg mixture into the flour mixture.

Using a spoon, divide the mixture between the loaf tins.

5. BAKE

Place them in the preheated oven for 20–25 minutes.

VARIATIONS

Use dates instead of chocolate.

Add a spoon of sugar if you need them a little sweeter.

If you cannot get your hands on mini loaf tins, use a muffin tin, just grease round with some margarine to stop them sticking.

Baked

SHAPED BISCUITS

Rub, rub, rub

This is a lovely mixture for making all different shapes of biscuits: gingerbread men, farm animals, Christmas shapes, Halloween shapes (or any occasion) – just choose a cutter.

INGREDIENTS

75g PLAIN FLOUR

150g SELF-RAISING FLOUR

75g BUTTER

75g SOFT BROWN SUGAR

1 TEASPOON OF GINGER or MIXED SPICE

1 EGG

1 TABLESPOON SYRUP

DECORATIONS: icing, sprinkles, silver balls, sweets, liquorice – anything you like!

HOW TO MAKE

1. PREPARATION

Preheat the oven to gas 4 or 180°c (fan 160°c).

Line a baking tray with greaseproof paper.

Collect the cutters you would like to use.

2. MAKE THE DRY MIX

Place the plain and self-raising flour into the same bowl.

Chop the butter into cubes and add it into the flour.

Rub, rub, rub the butter into the flour with your fingertips until the mix looks like breadcrumbs.

Add in the sugar and ginger or mixed spice.

3. MAKE THE WET MIX

Crack the egg into a jug and beat it with a fork.

Measure the syrup into the egg and mix well.

Cut

Smile

4. MAKE THE DOUGH

Now add the wet mixture to the dry mixture and stir well.

Get your hands in the mixture to pull it all together.

TIP: If you have time, wrap the dough in some cling film and place in the fridge for 30 minutes to chill. This will make it easier to roll out.

5. BISCUIT MAKING

Flour the worktop and split the dough into 4 pieces.

Place one piece on the flour and sprinkle some flour on the top.

Very gently roll this piece out to the thickness of a pound coin.

Take your cutter and cut out your shapes.

Add your remnants to one of the other 3 pieces, roll out again, and keep repeating the process until you run out of dough!

Place the shapes onto a baking tray.

6. BAKE

Place in the preheated oven and bake for 20 minutes.

Take out and leave to cool on the baking tray.

TIP: If the shapes are different sizes they won't all require the same cooking time, so bake smaller biscuits all together and larger ones all together (for example, on different baking trays). This way the biscuits shouldn't burn.

7. DECORATE

Once cooled, decorate any way you like – no two will ever be the same!

THANK YOU

To all the people who have joined in the Mrs Bun the Baker baking classes, from toddlers through to adults, I love teaching you all. My Mum for teaching me the essential baking skills; Dad for being you; Bruv for tirelessly working with me on the book; my son Freddie for being my first guinea pig to teach and inspiring me to teach others; Hubby for just always being there and believing in me that I could do this, supporting me all the way.

info@mrsbunthebaker.net
www.mrsbunthebaker.net

 www.facebook.com/mrsbunthebaker
 @AMrsbunthebaker
 mrsbunthebaker

ISBN 978-1-5272-2566-4

© 2018 Angela Johnson trading as Mrs Bun the Baker®
First published 2015. Revised and expanded 2018.

The right of Angela Johnson, trading as Mrs Bun the Baker® to be identified as the author of this work has been asserted by her in accordance with the copyright, design and patents act 1988. All rights reserved. No part of this book may be reproduced, stored in a retrieval system, or transmitted, in any form or by any means, electronic, mechanical, photocopying, recording or otherwise, without the prior permission of the publisher.

Design: ian@eandp.co.uk